FIRST STEP

TAKE YOUR BOX
of crayons and
DUMP THEM OUT

ALL WORKING PAGE

NUMBERS ARE ON

THE BOTTOM RIGHT

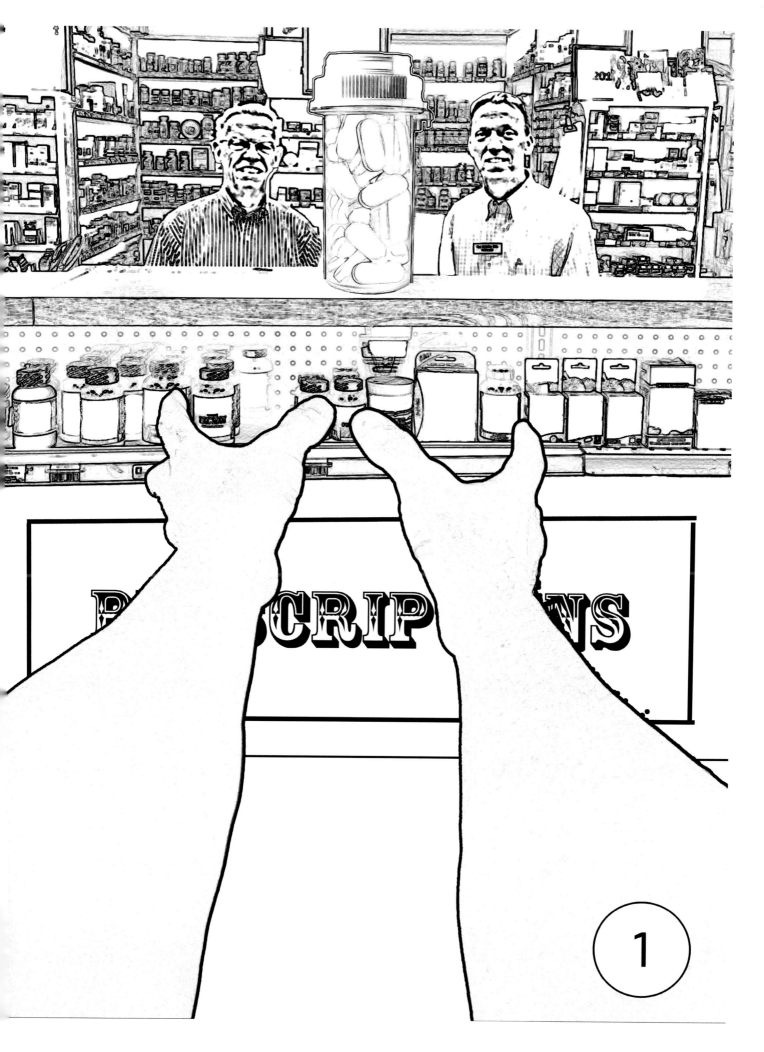

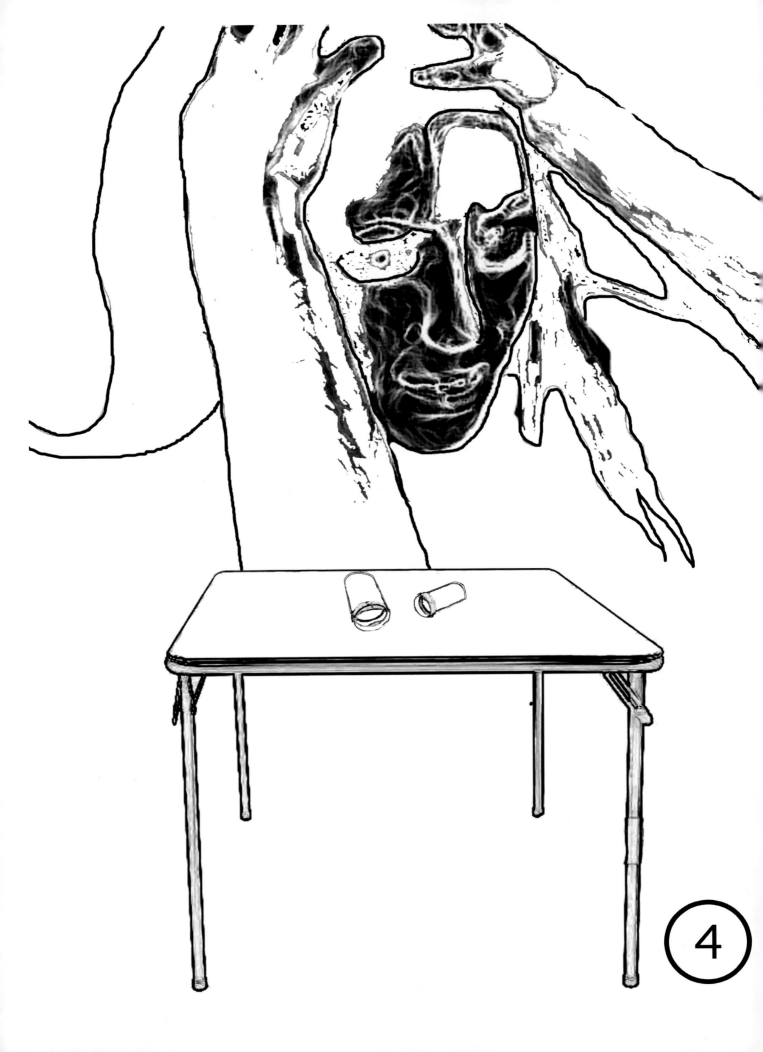

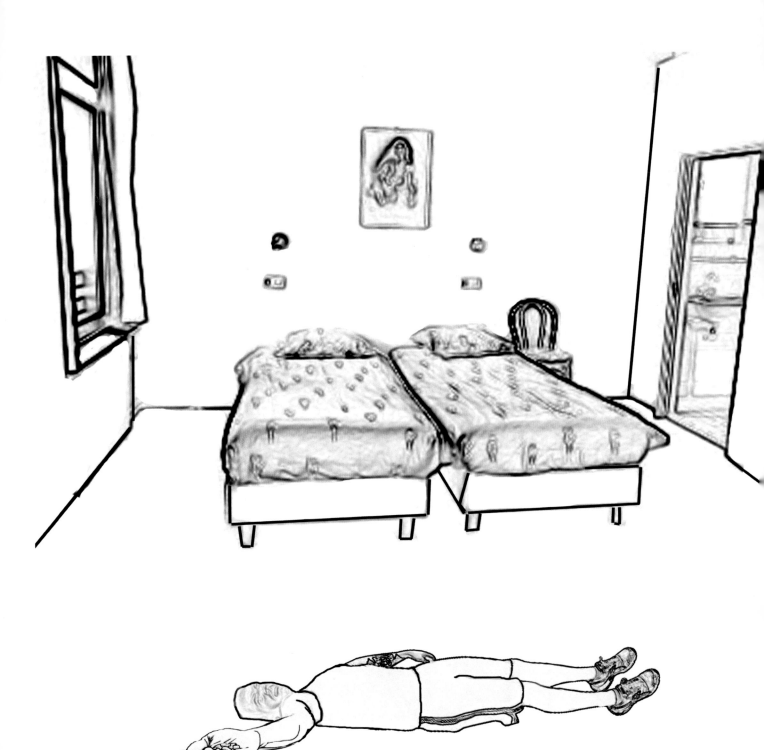

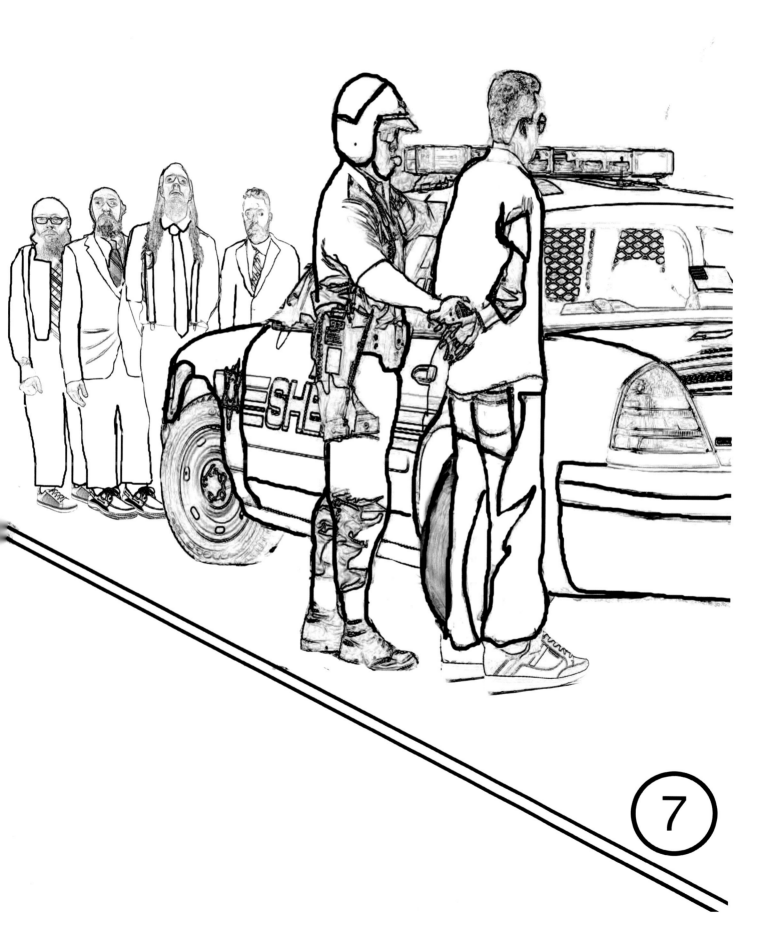

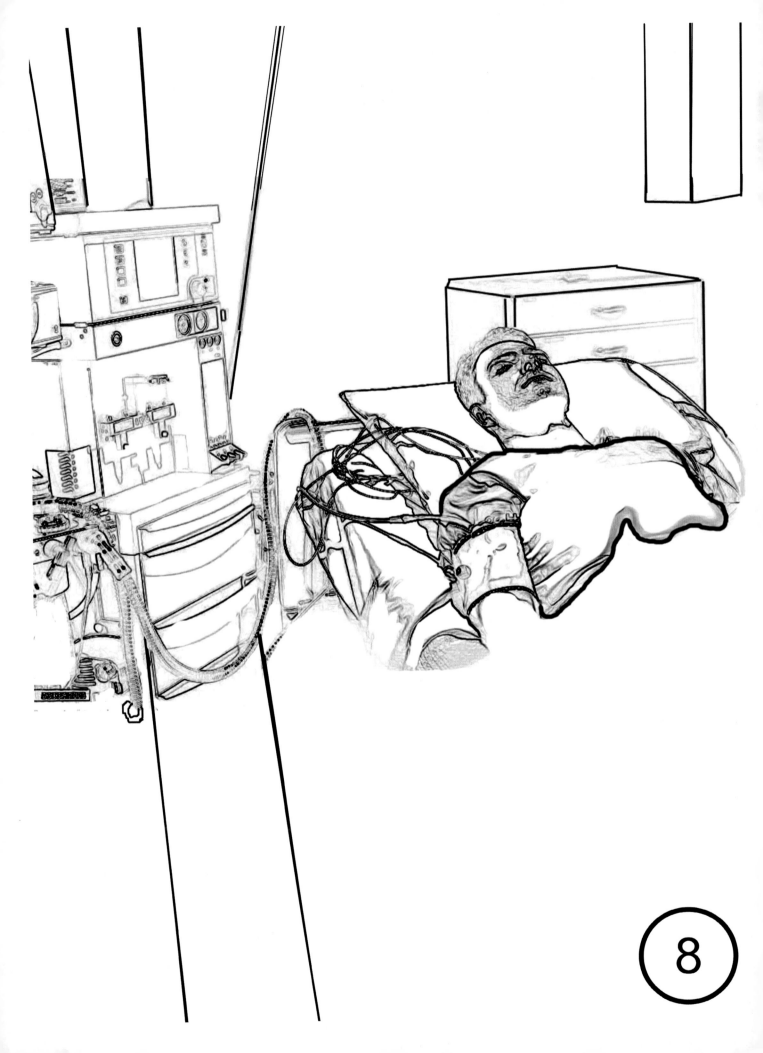

COURTHOUSE

14

Addiction Treatment Center

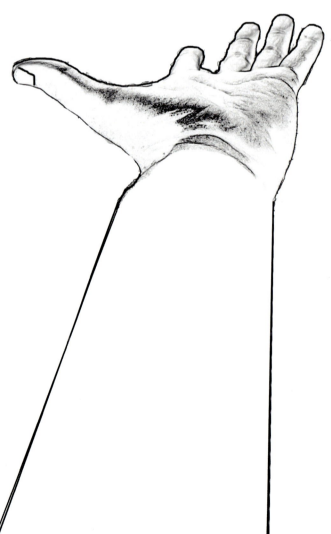

18

AREAS OF INTEREST

WITH YOUR FINISHED PAGE, COMPARE THE COLORS USED TO THE FEELINGS THEY REPRESENT. TAKE FOR INSTANCE, AN OBJECT OR AREA COLORED WITH THE SCARLET COLOR WOULD MEAN, THE AREA OR OBJEST IS BEWILDERING TO YOU. CHECK ALL AREAS TO SEE WHAT MAKES YOU MAD TO HAPPY (YOUR FRIENDS OR THERAPIST MAY HAVE TO HELP WITH YOUR RESULTS)

COLORS USED	FEELING REPRESENTED
BLACK	ANGER
PURPLE	RESENTED
BLUE-VIOLET	IRRITATED
BLUE	DISTURBED
BROWN	UNEASY
GRAY	SAD
SCARLET	BEWILDERED
VIOLET-RED	HELPLESS
GREEN	WORRIED
YELLOW-GREEN	OVERWHELMED
WHITE	FRUSTRATED
INDIGO	NATURAL
CERULEAN	WORTHY
BLUE-GREEN	INDIFFER
RED-VIOLET	CONTENT
RED	CALM
GREEN-YELLOW	ELATED
CARNATION	GLAD
DANDELION	HAPPY
APRICOT	EXCITED
YELLOW-ORANGE	JOYFUL
ORANGE	OVERJOYED
RED-ORANGE	PLEASED
YELLOW	WONDERFUL

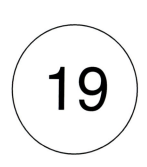

FOR EACH COLOR USED, ADD CORRESPONDING NUMBER

BLACK	1
PURPLE	2
BLUE-VIOLET	3
BLUE	4
BROWN	5
GRAY	6
SCARLET	7
VIOLET-RED	8
GREEN	9
YELLOW-GREEN	10
WHITE	11
INDIGO	12
CERULEAN	13
BLUE-GREEN	14
RED-VIOLET	15
RED	16
GREEN-YELLOW	17
CARNATION	18
DANDELION	19
APRICOT	20
YELLOW-ORANGE	21
ORANGE	22
RED-ORANGE	23
YELLOW	24

A HIGH SCORE (83)
A MEDIUM SCORE (45)
A LOW SCORE (20)

Choose the score level closest to your total.

HIGH SCORE (The picture you have chosen to color is pleasant topic for you)

MEDIUM SCORE (the picture you have chosen to color is a topic you are indifferent to)

LOW SCORE (The picture you have chosen to color is slightly depressing for you)

EACH SCORE LEVEL HAS DIFFERENT DEGREES OF FEELINGS DEPENDING ON HOW CLOSE OR FAR YOUR TOTOL IS TO THEIR SCORE RANGE.

TAKE FOR INSTANCE, YOUR SCORE IS (15) YOU ARE MORE DEPRESSED WITH THE CHOCEN TOPIC

PAGES CHOSEN

PAGES

1   (Liberated) Your at the right place you think.
        (Life couldn't be better)

2   (Comfortable) A quiet place
        (Enjoying a time with friends)

3   (Optimistic) Finding what you need.
        (Could be the last)

4   (Enraged) Just ran out.
        (Your mind starts to find a way for more)

5   (Paranoid) Who or what is there?
        (Your thoughts are uncontrollable)

6   (Overdose) Just one more.
        (Not wasting time can kill you)

7   (Embarrassed) Just a bad break.
        (You'll get over it soon)

8   (Unlucky) Just a small mistake.
        (You will know what to look for the next time)

9   (Hesitant) Looking into the future.
        (Is it all worth it ?)

10   (Powerless) A new morning.
        (Only brings memories of the past)

11   (Perplexed) It keeps happening.
        (You might think you have a problem)

12   (Unpleasant) A period of time.
        (What has to be done)

13   (Tormented) Slow walk fast train.
        (Life is losing its grip)

14   (Threatened) He seems unfair.
        (Court system is winning)

15   (Desperate) A day of shopping.
        (Anything to eat or sell)

16   (Wonderful) Big score.
        (Life is tolerable today)

17   (Doubtful) Going to work.
        (The only job left)

18   (Skeptical) Treatment is everywhere.
        (Whats the excuse today ?)

NOTES

Made in the USA
Columbia, SC
20 April 2020